in a Garden

by Sara Flannery

SCHOOL PUBLISHERS

Cover, p.3, p.14, ©Harcourt; p.4, p.7, ©David Young-Wolff/PhotoEdit; p.5, p.8, ©HARCOURT; p.6, ©CORBIS; p.9, (tc) (bc) (br) ©Artville, (bl) (tr) ©Corel, (tl) ©PhotoDisc; p.10, ©Digital Vision/Punch Stock; p.11, ©PhotoDisc; p.12, ©ThinkStock/Index Stock; p.13, ©CORBIS/Punch Stock.

Printed in China

ISBN 10: 0-15-350666-0
ISBN 13: 978-0-15-350666-6

Ordering Options
ISBN 10: 0-15-350600-8 (Grade 3 On-Level Collection)
ISBN 13: 978-0-15-350600-0 (Grade 3 On-Level Collection)
ISBN 10: 0-15-357859-9 (package of 5)
ISBN 13: 978-0-15-357859-5 (package of 5)

1 2 3 4 5 6 7 8 9 10 985 12 11 10 09 08 07 06

A Garden Grows

Alice Waters drove past the school every day, and the sight made her sad. The windows were dark, and they were marked up. The grass was burnt and dry.

Ms. Waters used to be a teacher, so she worried about the school. Ms. Waters is not just a worried ex-teacher, however. She is an important chef who owns a famous restaurant in Berkeley, California.

Ms.Waters believes in using good, fresh food. Her restaurant uses local resources. She wants food to be healthy and delicious.

One day, a reporter asked Ms. Waters about education. She talked about the sad-looking school.

Neil Smith was the principal of that school. When he read Ms.Waters' words he called her, and Ms. Waters suggested a garden.

The students would plant seeds and watch them grow. They would learn about taking care of their plants, and the garden would teach them about nature. Best of all, it would be a source of good food.

Teachers and students cleaned up the empty lot next to the school. They put in plants that would feed the soil.

Then the school hired a cooking teacher. The teacher fixed up the old cafeteria, which became a huge kitchen. Soon kids were taking cooking classes.

Within the year, the garden was growing! Every year, the garden grew bigger. The garden was now part of the school's culture.

Meet the Garden

The garden is part of the school's science classes. Each fall, a new class learns about the garden. First the class meets the garden manager.

The manager acts as a tutor for the class. The manager tells the class how to respect the garden, and then the class explores. The students smell different plants, they taste ripe fruit, and they sample the vegetables.

They pick corn, roast it, and eat it. The delicious corn was planted last spring as a welcome to the new class.

The students each choose a special spot in the garden. They can go there during class and write about what they see and hear and think.

They are given information about garden tools. They learn how to take care of them. They find out how to clean up.

A Day in the Garden

Each garden class begins with a meeting. The garden manager tells about that day's chores. The manager also asks a question. Students may be asked to find a certain type of plant, or to imagine a plant superhero. Students think about the question during class that day.

Students then pick jobs and work in small groups. A garden teacher or volunteer goes with each group. The students figure out what tools they will need, and then they get the tools from the tool shed.

The tool shed also has coats, gloves, and boots. These "garden uniforms" help keep clothes and shoes clean.

Some groups may plant seeds, some may weed, and others may pick ripe fruit. Plants often need to be watered. Leaves and grass are gathered because as they rot, they help feed the soil.

The garden changes each season. In the winter, classes plant carrots, beets, and peas. In spring, they plant peppers, corn, and some berries. They plant garlic, onions, and clover in the fall.

The garden also has apple, plum, and fig trees. Students may sample any of the delicious fruits and vegetables they find. Smelling and tasting is part of class.

A chicken coop was added a couple of years ago. The chickens stay there at night and walk in the garden during the day. The class takes care of the chickens, and the chickens provide fresh eggs.

Some cooking is done right in the garden. There is a small stove where eggs or some vegetables can be cooked. There is a larger wood-burning stove that is used to bake fresh pizza!

When a bell rings, it is time to clean up. The groups clean all the tools and put them where they belong. Then the students gather in a circle. They talk about the day's work and answer the day's question.

In the Kitchen

Kids have learned how to grow food. Kitchen classes give them information on how to turn the food into meals.

The class learns how to use the kitchen equipment. They experiment with the mixer. They learn the safe way to prepare food. They find out how to clean up after cooking.

Kitchen classes always begin the same way. Students wash their hands, put on aprons, and then they gather around a big table. They hear about what delicious food they will make that day.

The class breaks into groups, and each group prepares a part of the meal. The students use what is ripe in the garden at that time. They may make soup or salad, or they may grind corn into flour.

Tables are set with cloths, and everyone has plates and silverware. Flowers from the garden are placed on each table. The class enjoys the food together.

Then it's time to clean up. Dishes are washed, tables are wiped, and leftovers are used to feed the soil in the garden.

The Future

Ms. Waters' garden idea changed one school. Now she wants to change others. Waters instructs other schools on how to start gardens and about eating better.

People often eat without thinking. They don't know where their food comes from. Growing a garden can change that. Kids grow their own food, cook it, and are proud of what they make! Food is science, food is history, and food is art. A garden is a wonderful school.

Think Critically

1. Why does Alice Waters know so much about food?

2. How does the garden help the school?

3. What part of the story would you look at to find out what students do in each garden class?

4. How is the garden manager a tutor for the students?

5. Would you prefer to work in the garden or in the kitchen? Why?

Social Studies

Community Garden A community garden is a great way for neighbors to work together and to cooperate. It is also a great way to grow delicious food! Find out whether there is a community garden in your area. If there is, research how to become involved. If there is not, find out how you might start one.

School-Home Connection Ask everyone in your family to name a favorite fruit and vegetable. Have them tell why they like them. Think about your favorite choices. Then make something to eat together.

Word Count: 936